HOW TO BE THE SPOUSE
GOD WANTS YOU TO BE

Male and Female Created He Them

KDP

How to Be the Spouse God Wants You to Be
Male and Female Created He Them

Cover Photograph: Faye and Tom Dawdy
Design and Layout: Amy Paige
Editor: Frances Mosher

Library of Congress Catalogue
Hodges, Zane C., 1932-2008
ISBN 9798730340046

Contents

Foreword

In 1998 at the age of 65-66, Zane Hodges taught the following messages on marriage at the Lord's Supper meetings at Victor Street Bible Chapel, where Zane ministered for about 50 years. Zane was also a professor of New Testament Greek at Dallas Theological Seminary from 1959-1986. Zane never married and was a lifelong bachelor when he went home to be with the Lord in 2008.

Now, a fair question to ask is "How much insight on marriage could possibly come from a 65-year-old man who never married?" Such a person has no personal experience to share. However, if the question is "What does the Bible teach about marriage?", then the answer does not depend on personal experiences, but on the understanding of the Bible. We invite you to evaluate Zane's insights on marriage, based on the Word of God.

For many years, Zane provided marital counseling for many couples and this book mentions some of those experiences. However, we were struck by how little Zane focused on this and how much he focused on the Bible, especially the Creation account in Genesis 2:15-3:13. Whenever insights are drawn directly from the Bible, we remember the words of the LORD in Isaiah 55:11--

So shall My word be that goes forth from My mouth;
It shall not return to Me void,
But it shall accomplish what I please,
And it shall prosper in the thing for which I sent it.

For those who are married and for those who are considering marriage, we hope you will be blessed as we were from this book.

Letitia and Michael Lii
Victor Street Bible Chapel
March 18, 2021

Chapter 1
The Woman Who Wrecked the World

There is an old saying: "Fools rush in where angels fear to tread." My addressing the subject of marriage might tempt some to think of a variation on that: Bachelors rush in where married men fear to tread. [1] However, I don't think the two statements are really parallel because, first of all, married men are not angels. Just ask a woman who's married to one, and I assure you that she will tell you she's not married to an angel. I have the opinion that married men, deep down in their hearts, do not think bachelors are necessarily fools! So I make no apology for attempting this, as long as I can keep my focus on the Word of God.

In fact, the case can be made that God, perhaps, thinks it's a little better for us to get marital counsel from an unmarried person than from a married person. The New Testament epistles, which basically teach us what we need to know for the Christian life, were written by five men: James, John, Jude, Peter, and Paul. Of the five writers, James, John, and Jude say nothing about marriage -- nothing. Peter, who wrote two epistles, gives six verses to marriage, and I've always been a little amused by the fact that he gives one verse to husbands and five verses to wives. But the Apostle Paul beats them all the way around by giving the vast majority of the Bible's marital instruction. In addition to the famous passage in Ephesians 5, which is so frequently read at weddings, 1 Corinthians 7 is a very long chapter dealing with various aspects of marriage, and there are other references to marriage in the Pauline Epistles. Now, I realize that some people have thought Paul might have been a widower. We know he was not married at the time of the writing of 1 Corinthians, and I'm unaware of any really good evidence even suggesting he was ever married. If he had been married and became a widower, he does a very good job of hiding it from us. So as far as we know, we are getting the majority of the Bible's marital counsel from a man who is not -- and probably was not ever -- married. We're going to be looking at Paul's advice and at the other biblical advice as well.

---

[1] Zane gave these series of messages at the Lord's Supper meetings at Victor StreetBible Chapel in 1998. Zane was a lifelong bachelor and was 65-66 years old when he gave these messages.

Now those who know me know, that I have engaged in marital counsel for many years. I've lost track of the number of husbands, wives, and husbands and wives together that I've talked to. Those who have had any exposure to me as a marital counselor are probably aware that I usually come down a little harder on the man than on the woman. One of the reasons for that is that God makes the man the head of the home, and therefore he has the most serious responsibility. But this chapter is going to address the ladies. I will be getting around to the men in subsequent chapters, but I'm going to start by concentrating on the ladies and am titling this chapter "The Woman Who Wrecked the World." (Now you can understand why no married man is likely to use a title like that.) I don't even need to tell you what the woman's name was, do I? You know what her name was. We're going to read about her in Genesis.

But first, I want to look at 1 Timothy 2:11-14. The Apostle Paul writing:

Let a woman learn in silence with all submission. And I do not permit a woman to teach or to have authority over a man, but to be in silence.

For Adam was formed first, then Eve. And Adam was not deceived, but the woman being deceived, fell into transgression.

Now a lot of people, both men and women, have had trouble with some of the statements Paul has made about women. I know that some people have even suggested he wrote these things because he didn't like women; he hated women; and he wanted to put them in their place. We obviously know that was not true of the Apostle Paul, who wrote not only as a servant of God, but under the inspiration of Scripture. Other people take another and more indirect approach to it, and say, "Well, Paul was influenced by the culture of his time, and in the Jewish culture, as well as in the Gentile culture of his day, the woman had a very secondary position. It simply reflects the opinions and attitudes of his culture. We need to update his opinions and to bring them into the twentieth century." Now I think you can see -- if you believe the Bible is the inspired Word of God and the product, ultimately, of the Holy Spirit -- then that doesn't wash as an explanation for Paul's statements. Reread 1 Timothy 2:12, where Paul says, "I do not permit a woman to teach or to have authority over a man, but to be in silence -- because that's what our culture teaches us." Do you notice the italicized portion in your Bible? Of course not. It's not there!

Notice that Paul appeals first of all to the priority of man in Creation: "For Adam was first formed, then Eve" (v 13). Secondly, he appeals to the woman's role in the fall of man, and he says, "And Adam was not deceived [not a good note for Adam, I might add, because Adam sinned with his eyes wide open], but the woman being deceived, fell into transgression" (v 14). So what is Paul saying here? He's saying that because of the priority of man in Creation and because of the role that the woman played in the Fall: "I do not permit a woman to teach, or to have authority over the man, but to be in silence" (v 12). This is talking about the main church meeting (Lord Supper meeting) [2] as far as the biblical pattern is concerned. If women have ever wondered why they don't speak at the main meeting in churches seeking to follow the biblical pattern, this verse is one of the reasons why.

Now obviously this passage directs us back to the central passage I want to discuss, Genesis, chapters 2 and 3. I'll begin with Genesis 2:7-9:

> And the LORD God formed man of the dust of the ground, and
> breathed into his nostrils the breath of life; and man became a living
> being. The LORD God planted a garden eastward in Eden, and
> there He put the man whom He had
> formed. And out of the ground the LORD God made every tree
> grow that is pleasant to the sight and good for food. The tree of life
> was also in the midst of the garden, and the tree of the knowledge
> of good and evil.

Now notice here, there are some very basic and simple facts. God creates the man, He plants a garden for the man to live in, and He fills this garden with every kind of tree that was good for food and that was beautiful. And notice that it says here, "The tree of life was in the midst of the garden, and the tree of the knowledge of good and evil" (v 9), was there as well. Now, skipping down to verses 15-17:

> Then the LORD God took the man and put him in the garden of
> Eden to tend [the word tend here means something like to cultivate]
> and keep it. And the LORD God commanded the man, saying,

---

[2] 1 Corinthians 11:17-33. Victor Street Bible Chapel weekly observes the Lord's Supper by reading of Scripture, breaking of bread, Bible discussion among the men during a meal, and drinking of the fruit of the vine.

"Of every tree of the garden you may freely eat; but of the tree of

the knowledge of good and evil, you shall not eat, for in the day that

you eat of it you shall surely die."

Now this is a very important set-up passage for the thrust of this chapter. The man has been created. He has been placed in this garden with all these lovely trees as well as all these excellent fruits, but he is not placed there just to live out his years. He is given a job, and his job is expressed in verse 15: He is to tend the garden and keep it. He's to cultivate the garden and keep it. Now he has a positive responsibility and a negative responsibility. The positive responsibility is, "Keep the garden tended." The negative responsibility is, "Don't eat of the tree of the knowledge of good and evil." This is a very simple program, couldn't we admit? But that was what his job was: to take care of the garden and to avoid eating of the tree of the knowledge of good and evil.

Now this brings us to the creation of the woman and man's subsequent fall, found in Genesis 2:18-3:7:

And the LORD God said, "It is not good that man should be alone;

I will make him a helper comparable to him." Out of the ground the

LORD God formed every beast of the field and every bird of the air,

and brought them to Adam to see what he would name them. And

whatever Adam called each living creature, that was its name. So

Adam gave names to all cattle, to the birds of the air, and to every

beast of the field. But for Adam there was not found a helper compa-

rable to him. And the LORD God caused a deep sleep to fall on Adam,

and he slept; and He took one of his ribs, and closed up the flesh in

its place. Then the rib which the LORD God had taken from man He

made into a woman, and He brought her to the man. And Adam said:

"This is now bone of my bones And flesh of my flesh;

She shall be called Woman,

Because she was taken out of Man."

Therefore a man shall leave his father and mother and be joined to his wife,

and they shall become one flesh. And they were both naked, the man
and his wife, and were not ashamed.

Now the serpent was more cunning than any beast of the field which the LORD
God had made. And he said to the woman, "Has God indeed said,
'You shall not eat of every tree of the garden'?" And the woman said to the
serpent, "We may eat the fruit of the trees of the garden; but of the fruit of
the tree which is in the midst of the garden, God has said, 'You shall not eat it,
nor shall you touch it, lest you die.' " Then the serpent said to the woman, "You
will not surely die. For God knows that in the day you eat of it your eyes will be
opened, and you will be like God, knowing good and evil." So when the
woman saw that the tree was good for food, that it was pleasant to the eyes, and
a tree desirable to make one wise, she took of its fruit and ate. She also
gave to her husband with her, and he ate. Then the eyes of both of them
were opened, and they knew that they were naked; and they sewed fig leaves
together and made themselves coverings.

All right, we've got the scene: Man has been created and placed in this lovely
garden, and
his responsibility is to take care of the garden and to avoid eating of the tree of the
knowledge of good and evil. God surveys the scene and He says, "It is not good that
man should be alone. I will make someone who will love him." Genesis 2:18 doesn't
say that, does it? "It is not good that man should be alone. I will make somebody for
him to talk to." No, it doesn't say that. "It is not good for man to be alone. I will make
somebody who will comfort him and keep him company." No, it doesn't say that.
What God says is: "It is not good that man should be alone. I will make a helper
comparable to him" (2:18).

Now, please do not think that the word "helper" implies that the woman has
some kind of inferior status. It may interest you to know that the word helper used
here is also used in a number of the Psalms to refer to the help of God, or to God
as a Helper. Psalm 33:20 says, "Our soul waits for the LORD; He is our help [or,
He is our Helper] and our shield." It seems to me that even though we must, on the
basis of the Bible, say that God created the woman to be man's helper, we must also

say that, because God Himself is a Helper, this is a very high and noble role He has given to the woman. Which of us does not want the help of God? All of us want God to help us when we need help. That's one of the roles that God has in each and every life, male and female. If you're a man, God is your Helper. If you're a woman, God is your Helper. That's a high model, and that's what the woman was created to do for the man -- to be his helper.

Now we're not talking about somebody to fix the meals. Did you notice that there were no meals to fix in the Garden of Eden? They just ate the fruit. We're not talking here about somebody to take the dirty clothes to the laundromat. There were no dirty clothes in the Garden of Eden (in fact, originally, no clothes at all), so that was not the woman's role. We're not talking about somebody to clean up the house or sweep out all the dirt. There is no house in the Garden of Eden.

Then, what are we talking about? Well, God has just said to the man, "Take care of the garden, cultivate the garden." And then He says, "It is not good for man to be alone in the tasks that I have given him. I'll make somebody to help him with his tasks." May I suggest that the highest goal of a wife is to help her husband be the man God wants him to be and to do the things that God wants him to do? If that is not the role a wife is fulfilling in the life of her husband, she has yet to learn what it means to be a wife.

It would be interesting to ask each wife in a group of Christian married people why she married the man she married. I suspect we would get a variety of answers. One answer might be, "I married this guy because I was really in love with him and wanted to spend the rest of my life with him." (She may have had second thoughts since then, but that may have been the original reason.) Another might say, "The reason I married this man is that I wanted to establish a home, have children, and raise a family." But I wonder how many, at the time they got married, would have said, "The reason I'm marrying this man is so that I can help him to be the man that God wants him to be." Do you know what I bet? There might not be a single wife in the group who thought of it like that when they got married. Well, if you've never thought of it like that, start thinking of it like that. "It is not good for a man to be alone. I will make him a helper. I have given him a job to do, and I want somebody to help him to do it."

14

But that brings us to the temptation, doesn't it? That brings us to the story of the Fall. You'll notice that in Genesis 3 we are told that the serpent through whom, obviously, the devil was working "was more cunning than any beast of the field, which the LORD God had made" (v 1). The serpent was very clever, says this text, very clever. So does the text say, "The serpent was more cunning than any beast of the field which the Lord God had made, and the serpent said to the man. . ."? No! The serpent was smart, so he talked to the woman.

When you hear some people discuss marriage, you can very easily get the impression that the vast majority of problems in marriages come from husbands: "If my husband were only this or that or this other thing, then our marriage would really be great." "The devil works in our marriage through my husband, and he fouls things up." Well, I've got a news flash for you! The devil is capable of working in marriages through the woman, and when the woman forgets the role for which God made her, believe me, the devil will take advantage of that in a big way.

So Satan approaches the woman, and he says to the woman, "Has God indeed said, 'You shall not eat of every tree of the garden'?" (v 1). Notice how Satan phrases that for the woman. Let's translate that into modern language: "Has God really said 'you can't have it all'? 'You can't have it all' -- Is that what God has said to you?" How many women are susceptible to that? You know, it's really surprising how often a woman will get to the state where she's surrounded by all sorts of privileges that other women would kill to get, and she says, "We don't have this," "My husband doesn't do that," or, "My life is missing that particular thing." One of the things that the devil can do with considerable success with women is to focus them on what they do not have. Notice what the woman's answer here is:

> And the woman said to the serpent, "We may eat the fruit of the trees
> of the garden, but of the fruit of the tree which is in the midst of the
> garden,
> God has said, 'You shall not eat it, nor shall you touch it, lest you die' "
> (vv 2,3).

Wait a minute. I thought the earlier verse said that the tree of life was in the midst of the garden. What happened to the tree of life here? She ignores it. What's in the middle of the garden for the woman at this moment? You know what's in the middle of her garden. It's what she can't have. That's what's in the middle of her garden. "We can eat of the trees," she said, "but that tree that's right in the heart of the garden that we pass by all the time, you know, and I've looked at it..." -- I'm elaborating here -- "That thing that's in the midst of the garden, I can't have it. I can't have it." And she says, "The reason I can't have it is because God says that when I eat it, I'll die."

The devil says, "Oh no, you won't die. Don't be silly. You're not going to die if you eat of that tree. Because God knows that in the day that you eat, your eyes will be opened, you'll be like God knowing good and evil. Oh, you're missing something," says the devil. "You are really, really, really missing something. The tree that God has forbidden you to have is the one that, first of all, will open your eyes and will make you like God, knowing good and evil."

Notice that the woman, first of all, is focused on what she doesn't have, and secondly on how good it would be to have what she doesn't have. But if God didn't give it to her, it wasn't good for her, right? The devil can, first of all, focus a wife on one particular thing that she doesn't have, that seems very nice and then persuade her that she is missing so much by not having it. When a woman is persuaded of that by the devil, she no longer thinks in terms of her role in the marriage as a helper.

Now notice what happens next. The woman looks at the tree. You know what she sees? Not a tree that will kill her. Not a tree that will break her relationship with God. Not even a tree that could possibly break her relationship with her husband. What if he doesn't eat of it and she does? She doesn't see the tree that way anymore. You know what she sees in that tree? She sees delicious fruit, beautiful fruit, and a tree that is "desirable to make one wise" (v6). "Oh, I just have got to have that." She took of it and ate.

What was she doing? Was she helping her husband? No. She was acting selfishly. She wasn't thinking of anything at that moment except what she wanted. As I have mentioned, I have counseled husbands and wives together and separately more times than I can enumerate. And after hearing both sides, do you know what I usually say to myself? "This problem could be easily solved if both of them would be less selfish."

Almost always, especially in Christian marriages, when something goes wrong, at least one person is selfish. That is the avenue through which the devil entered the first marriage in human history. He got the woman focused on what she didn't have, and she began to think about it selfishly.

The next phrase is short, but devastating: "...she took of its fruit and ate. She also gave to her husband with her, and he ate" (vv 6,7). This is the helper, folks! This is the being that God created to help the man, to help him meet his responsibilities, and to help him be what God wanted him to be in the garden. What does she do? She helps him break his relationship with God.

They lose their home in the garden because they are driven out of the garden. Both of them are made subject to death. When a wife forgets her role as the helper of her husband and when she begins to act selfishly, what is she doing? She is threatening her home, her marriage, her children, and her happiness.

Is there any woman reading this who thinks she can be happy without fulfilling God's purpose for her? Is there any woman reading this who would say, "Well Zane, maybe God did make women to be helpers, but I don't really like that role, and my husband doesn't really deserve that from me. If you knew what kind of husband I was married to and how much help he needed, you wouldn't be so complacent. So I'm not going do it God's way. I'm not going to be the kind of wife that God designed me to be." Do you think you're going to be happy? Think again. That's a fantasy. Neither the man nor the woman can be truly happy or fulfilled unless they are happy in accordance with the way God has created them to be. If all Christian married couples understood that, we would have a lot fewer difficulties in Christian marriages.

All professors and ex-professors give tests[3]. This test is for the wives who are reading this. (Men can rate their wives, but don't you dare tell them how you rated them. I don't want you to get in trouble, and I don't want to get in trouble, either!) Which of the following three statements best characterizes your role as a helper of your husband?

A: My husband would be a better Christian man if he was married to somebody besides me.

---

[3] Zane was a New Testament professor at Dallas Theological Seminary, 1959-1986.

B: My husband's Christian life and service is his own business. That's his thing. I'm doing my thing.

C: I am fully committed, by the grace of God, to helping my husband be the best man he can possibly be for God.

Which of those three statements mostly describes your role in your relationship with your husband? If you chose A, give yourself a flunking grade, and a minus 100, because you are also saying, "Not only do I not help my husband, but I'm a hindrance to him. " If you chose B, give yourself a flunking grade, but this time you can take a zero, because you're saying, "I neither help nor hinder him." I hope you chose C--or if you couldn't honestly choose it right now, that you have determined to choose it from now on. I hope you will choose to be deeply committed to helping your husband become the man that God wants him to become and to do the things that God wants him to do. Before seeking counseling for your marriage, first be sure you have that as your objective.

Now when I go into homes -- I guess I'd better admit this -- I'm always watching to see the dynamics between a husband and a wife. They may not know it, but I'm always doing that. Of course, I'm not expecting to see a big old fight with screaming and yelling because when the pastor comes calling, that's not what happens. Everybody's on their good behavior. So I'm not looking for something so obvious as that. I'm looking for little subtle things. I can't give you all my trade secrets, but let me tell you a few things.

I'm looking to see if, during the course of my visit, the husband and wife talk to each other a little bit as well as to me. And I'm interested in the tone of the exchange between them. If the husband and wife are not speaking at home, they may get past that by speaking only to me or mainly to me except as to say, "Pass the meat," or "Cut the bread," or something like that.

Another thing I'm looking for is whether, in the conversation, either of the spouses has a tendency to put the other one down, even with little gentle put-downs, such as, "Well my husband couldn't cut his way through a steak if his life depended on it." I remember years ago one of my heroes in baseball, Johnny Bench,[4] married a very attractive airline stewardess, and I read about it in the Cincinnati papers. They had both of them on camera and interviewed them. Some of the viewers who wrote to the newspaper said it was horrible because throughout the interview, the wife kept putting Johnny Bench down. Here is Cincinnati's hero, and she's there saying all sorts of negative things about him. The people who wrote to the newspaper said, "We don't expect this marriage to last very long." Sure enough, it didn't. They divorced.

I'm looking for little indications of whether the husband and wife respect each other. Here's another thing I'm looking for: I am looking to see if the wife is truly, truly interested in what her husband is doing for God. The writer of Proverbs, and with this I conclude, said, "Who can find a virtuous wife? For her worth is far above rubies. The heart of her husband safely trusts in her. . . She does him good and not evil all the days of her life" (Proverbs 31:10-11a; 12). Man, what a description for a wife! How fortunate a man is to find a virtuous wife. How fortunate a man is to find a woman that he can trust from day one to the end of life. How fortunate a man is to find a woman who will do "him good and not evil all the days of her life." That's a high standard, ladies, a high standard. And with the help of God, you can reach it.

---

[4] Baseball Hall of Fame catcher who played for the Cincinnati Reds, 1967-1983. The Cincinnati Reds were Zane's favorite baseball team.

Chapter 2
The Man Who Went Along to Get Along

We find the story of "The Man Who Went Along to Get Along" in Genesis 3:6-13:

> So when the woman saw that the tree was good for food, that it was
> pleasant to the eyes, and a tree desirable to make one wise, she took
> of its fruit and ate. She also gave to her husband with her, and he ate.
> Then the eyes of both of them were opened and they knew that they
> were naked; and they sewed fig leaves together and made themselves
> coverings.
> And they heard the sound of the Lord God walking in the garden
> in the cool of the day, and Adam and his wife hid themselves from
> the presence of the Lord God among the trees of the garden.
> Then the Lord God called to Adam and said to him, "Where are you?"
> So he said, "I heard Your voice in the garden, and I was afraid because
> I was naked; and I hid myself."
> And He said, "Who told you that you were naked? Have you eaten from
> the tree of which I commanded you that you should not eat?"
> Then the man said, "The woman whom You gave to be with me, she gave
> me of the tree, and I ate."
> And the Lord God said to the woman, "What is this you have done?"
> The woman said, "The serpent deceived me, and I ate."

As explained in Chapter 1, the biblical title for this book is Male and Female
Created He Them. I would like to note the fact that the Bible is not saying He
created them unisex. One of the problems in our culture and society today is that
people are allowing the breakdown of the created distinctions between men and
women. That's a fatal step to take and produces all kinds of difficulties. This is one
of the reasons I've gone back to the beginning of the account of the creation of man
and woman.

However, I could have chosen the more practical title: How to Get Along with Your Spouse. Once when I was teaching on this topic in a meeting, someone in the audience said, "I didn't know Zane had a spouse." So please notice that the title of this book is not How to Get Along with My Spouse, but How to Get Along with Your Spouse! I want to suggest that spouses do not get along well until they both accept the role God has given them in Creation, and that the secret of a happy marriage lies first and fundamentally in the willingness of the man to take the man's role and the woman to take the woman's role.

In the previous chapter, "The Woman Who Wrecked the World," I focused on Eve and the way in which the devil succeeded in getting her to eat of the tree of the knowledge of good and evil. The main point of Chapter 1 was that the woman was created to be man's helper, not in terms of doing the dishes, carrying out the garbage, or preparing the meals, but in helping the man to fulfill his responsibilities to God. Now there's an old saying, "You can take the teacher out of the school, but you can't take the school out of the teacher." I ended Chapter 1 with a quiz, and I'm tempted, at this point, to give a follow-up quiz to each married woman reading this. The quiz would ask her to list one, two, or three ways in which she is trying to improve her performance as someone who helps her husband to perform the will of God and to be a better servant of God.

This chapter addresses the men. One of the sad features of modern culture is that we have produced a lot of wife abusers. There are men who occasionally strike their wives, and there are men who frequently abuse their wives. When I find out that a man has struck his wife, my opinion of him sinks below zero. It seems to me that he's a coward, he's less than a man. It is inexcusable for any husband to strike his wife, no matter what the provocation. Men who do this periodically and regularly, sometimes beating their wives within an inch of their lives, are sick, in my opinion. A man like that is very sick and needs therapy. He needs the Lord, of course. But he also needs treatment because that kind of behavior is a sign of a very serious psychological and spiritual problem, as well as a serious addiction to violence. We must admit that one of the sad signs of the decay of our society is the increasing number of men who abuse their wives physically.

However, I want to suggest that the problem of most men is not that they are abusive husbands. The problem is that they are passive husbands. I suggest that for every man who is an abuser, there are probably five, six, seven or more men who are passive husbands. Now please understand that when I talk about a passive husband I'm not talking about the typical stereotype - the henpecked husband whose wife obviously wears the trousers in the family, she tells him what to do and he does it. This is the "Yes, dear" husband type. He says to his friends, "I always take a positive attitude toward my wife, always." And they say, "How come?" "Well," he says, "whenever she tells me to do something I say, 'Yes, dear. Yes, dear. Yes, dear.' "

There are some husbands like that, but that's not the type of husband this chapter will address. A man can be a passive husband in the sense I will be discussing, yet still be very stubborn and have a mind of his own. For example, he is comfortably seated in front of the television set watching the Dallas Cowboys football team or the Texas Rangers baseball team when the wife comes up and says, "Could you take me over to the mall so I can do some shopping?" He responds, "There's no way I'm going to go to the mall with you until the game is over." That's a very assertive response, but the man may still be a passive husband.

The kind of passivity I'm talking about is the husband who is passive regarding the spiritual welfare of his wife. I would like to suggest that many husbands display this kind of passivity because they are the sons of Adam. They behave as Genesis 3:6-12 tells us Adam behaved. Notice that after the serpent deceived the woman into taking a different look at the tree, we read that "when the woman saw that the tree was good for food, that it was pleasant to the eyes, and a tree desirable to make one wise, she took of its fruit and ate." (v 6). And then it says, "She also gave to her husband with her, and Adam said, 'No, no, sweetheart. (Now I don't really know whether Adam called Eve sweetheart. I just kind of like the term. All writers have to have a little license, so I'm going to pretend that Adam called Eve sweetheart.)

Adam said to Eve, "No, no, sweetheart. Do you realize that you are offering me a piece of fruit from the tree of the knowledge of good and evil, which God has commanded us never to eat of? Sweetheart, I can tell that you've already eaten because you have a half-eaten piece of fruit in your hand. I'm disturbed by this. This is a terrible, terrible mistake. The most important thing for us to do right now is to get it straightened out with God. When God begins to walk in the garden in the cool of the day, as He does every day, well, we're going to have to go into the garden, and you're going to have to tell God what you did. I'll be right there with you. I'll be right beside you, and we'll tell God that something awful has happened. We'll admit to this fault, and we'll see what God will do about it."

Of course, I'm making this up! Obviously, Adam didn't say anything like that, did he? Have you ever stopped to consider how different the history of mankind might have been if he had? But he didn't. Notice what the Scripture says; "she took of its fruit and ate. She also gave to her husband with her and he ate" (v 6). Just like that. Whew! As far as this record is concerned, no argument, no resistance. She gives the fruit to him, and he eats it.

Later on in the day the Lord is walking in the cool of the garden, and Adam and Eve, who have now felt shame over their nakedness, have put on some fig leaf aprons, and have hidden in the garden. God says, "Where are you, Adam?" (v 9)

Adam said, "I heard Your voice in the garden, and I was afraid because I was naked; and I hid myself." (v 10)

God said, "Who told you that you were naked? Have you eaten from the tree of which I commanded you that you should not eat?" (v 11)

Then comes the classic statement. Not only did sin start in the garden of Eden, but passing the buck started in the garden of Eden, too. Adam says, "The woman gave it to me." The buck is passed to Eve, but also to God: "The woman whom You gave to be with me, she gave me of the tree, and I ate" (v 12). Well, what do you know? "God, You're to blame. You gave me this woman. Now look what she's done to me."

Now don't think that men have never thought, felt, or spoken that way since the garden of Eden. "Lord, why in the world did You give me a wife like this? Why did You bring this woman into my life? Look how she's ripping my whole life apart." Of course, he's conveniently forgetting that when he married her, he thought she was the best thing this side of fried chicken. But when it goes wrong, "Ooh. Why did You do this to me?"

Now, Adam is passing the buck. I want you to see that clearly. Wouldn't you expect him to go on and say, "The woman whom You gave to be with me, she gave me of the fruit, and I said, 'No, no, no. I can't do this.' She said to me, 'Please do it.' She pleaded with me, begged me, and nagged me and nagged me and nagged me. She wouldn't speak to me for five hours. And finally, Lord, I couldn't take it anymore, and I ate."

You don't find that here, do you? But you better believe if he could have said it, he would have. He's already passing the blame to Eve. He's already passing the blame to God. But notice: "The woman whom You gave to be with me, she gave me of the tree, and I ate" (v 12). As simple and as easy as that. Adam can't say, "I resisted this. I pushed her away from me. I fought with her over this." No. "She gave me of the tree, and I ate."

You know, Adam is the world's number one pushover -- number one -- first, because he was the first man, and second because, as the New Testament says in 1 Timothy 2:14a, "And Adam was no deceived", he wasn't fooled by any of this. The woman was deceived by the serpent, but the man was not deceived. He knew what he was doing. Without the smallest amount of resistance, as far as the Scriptural record is concerned, he just went ahead and did it. Why?

Now, I want to make a suggestion, and in doing so I may run afoul of the male fraternity. It is my opinion that one of the greatest fears married men have is the fear of losing intimacy with their wives. Let me repeat that. I think one of the greatest fears married men have is the fear of losing intimacy with their wives -- personal intimacy and physical intimacy. Now, I don't find anything particularly wrong with the word sex, but I'm not going to use it here. Given the harsh overtones that the word sex sometimes has in the culture, I think it may be better to use the term physical intimacy. That is, after all, what God created in the marital relationship from the very beginning.

Now, I want you to think very carefully the position Adam was in at the moment his wife came up with this piece of fruit. You have got to put yourself in his place. Remember that Adam knew what it meant to be alone. For a while he was the only created human being, and remember that God said, "It is not good that man should be alone"[1]. God began to bring the animals He had created to man. Adam named all the animals, but not one of these animals was a suitable companion for him. God then made Adam go to sleep, and while Adam was asleep, God took out one of his ribs, and He created the first woman. When Adam woke up, there she was. I am sure she was marvelously beautiful -- perfect from head to toe.

They began a life of complete and total harmony. The only perfect marriage that has ever taken place on the face of the earth took place between Adam and Eve before the Fall. Think about it for a minute. They never fought. Neither partner was ever selfish. Eve would say, "What do you want to eat tonight, Adam?" Adam would reply, "Peaches. But what would you like to eat, Eve?" Eve may have answered, "Apples." So Adam said, "Let's do it your way." They never disagreed. Beyond all that, they had physical intimacy such as no two human beings have ever known in the history of the world. The intimacy and perfection of their relationship with each other day by day found its consummation and fulfillment in the physical intimacy that they were able to have with each other.

Now, remember that Eve had never known what it was to be alone. She was created when there was already a man there. But the man knew what it was like to be alone. When Eve came to Adam and said to him, "Here, eat this," for the very first time he was confronted with the possibility of creating a breach between himself and his wife, of having the first disagreement of their whole marital experience, and of giving her the first criticism that he had ever given her. Can you imagine this? He knew what it had been like to be alone, and he knew what it was like to be with this wonderful, wonderful, wonderful woman. When she said to him, "Eat of it," he

---

[1] Genesis 2:18

said, "Okay. Okay." He was not willing to risk the intimacy, the oneness, the union that he had with his wife in order to be obedient to God or, for that matter, to look out for Eve's interests.

So, what should he have done? He should certainly have said something like I suggested previously: "No, Eve, we can't. We'll have to go to God and talk about this. I don't know what this means for our relationship, but we have to get it straightened out with God." How do I know he should have done that? Because the model for married love that is given to us in the New Testament, and because the Modeler of married love is the Lord Jesus Christ, Himself. Ephesians 5:25-27a:

Husbands, love your wives, just as Christ also loved the church, and gave Himself for her; that He might sanctify and cleanse her with the washing of water by the word, that He might present her to Himself a glorious church, not having spot or wrinkle or any such thing.

What is the model for man's love for his wife? It is the love of Christ for the church. It is the love that drives the Lord Jesus Christ to sacrifice everything for the church.

And notice something in the above passage: The Lord Jesus Christ is not saying, "Oh well, I've saved her, I've justified her, and she's pretty good. I can live with that." No. He continues to work with her "that He might present her to Himself a glorious church, not having spot or wrinkle or any such thing" (v 27). The smallest imperfection in the church is a burden to Jesus Christ, the Head of the church. That, husbands, is the model for your love to your wife. Isn't it clear that when Adam took the fruit from Eve, he wasn't thinking of what was good for Eve? He was protecting himself. He was protecting the relationship that he thought he had to have.

Have you ever heard something like this? A man's friend says to him, "You know, I hate to tell you this. I don't like to talk about your wife, but she is a terrible gossip. She's gossiping all the time." The man says, "Yes, I know that. I've tried to bring it up once or twice, but every time I do, it ticks her off so bad, she burns the supper meat that night, and won't talk to me for three days. When it gets really bad, I sleep on the couch for a week. So I won't bring it up anymore. I don't talk to her about that. It's bad for the marriage." Is that the model of love?

Now guys, be very careful here. I don't want you sitting your wife down and saying, "Here are the spots and wrinkles in your Christian life that I think we need to deal with right away," because I don't want you later contacting me to say, "Zane, I took your advice, and she kicked me out of the house." Let me give you a piece of advice that Jesus gave about helping other people. Do you remember that Jesus said in Matthew 7: 3-5, "Why are you thinking about the little speck of wood in your brother's eye, and you're not paying attention to the log that is in your own eye? First," says Jesus, "cast the log out of your eye, and then you will see clearly to cast the speck out of your brother's eye." If you do what I suggested that you not do, more likely than your wife kicking you out of the house is that, when you have listed all the little specks in her spiritual life, she will list all the logs in your life. Chances are excellent that that could happen.

So what does that mean? It means, first of all: husbands, get your act together. Your model of behavior toward your wife is nothing less than the Lord Jesus Christ Himself. Your attitude, your tone of voice, your decisions -- everything -- have to be modeled on the character of the Savior. When you are behaving in a Christlike manner toward your wife, then God will be able to give you the skill, the wisdom, the love, and the grace to deal with the problems that she has in her spiritual life -- but probably not before that.

I'm very fond of the story about the grandmother who was being honored on her 60th wedding anniversary. During the course of the celebration a younger woman who was having trouble in her marriage approached the grandmother and said, "Tell me, what is the secret of your happy and enduring marriage?" The grandmother said, "Well, on the day I was married, I made up my mind that I would write down a list of ten faults of my husband which, for the sake of my marriage, I would overlook." So the younger woman said, "Well, tell me what were the ten faults of your husband that you wrote down?" The grandmother replied, "Well, to tell you the truth, I never got around to writing them down. But," she said, "every time my husband did something that made me hopping mad, I always said to myself,

'Lucky for him, that's one of the ten.' "

Now I hope that you guys are lucky enough to be married to a woman who does that. You probably need to be married to a woman that does that! (And I hope, by the way, wives, that you will do that.) Now let me tell you something. If I were married and I thought that my wife could sit down at the writing table and, in the blink of her eye, write down ten huge faults that I have, I should probably quit. Maybe I'm smart not to have married. But let me just tell you that if I thought my wife could do that, I would be horribly ashamed and embarrassed. I would feel that somehow or other, that I was not loving my wife as Christ loves the church. Get rid of the logs so that you can see clearly to help your wife.

I'll close the chapter with a story my mother told me. I believe she told me this story the last time I visited her. When my brother, David, and I were growing up, my dad had a grungy, ugly, dilapidated old cap that he liked to wear when he was working in the garden. Everybody in the family hated it except my father. So, as my mother told the story, one day my dad was out gardening and he had this cap on. She was at the sink, and from there she could look through the window and see him gardening. David came up to her and said, "Mother, I wish that Dad wouldn't wear that ugly old hat when he goes out into the garden. I hate that cap." My mother told me that she answered, "Yes, David, I know. But your father is so superior to other men that I think we can put up with a few things like that, don't you?" She reminded me of this story after my father had gone, after she had lived with him for 66 years. Did a husband ever get a better compliment than that? I wonder. I kind of doubt it. I will tell you that one of the greatest privileges I have ever had was being raised by a dad who was probably one of the most Christlike men I have ever known. I am lucky if I'm half as much like Christ as he was. Now, that was a man who could help his wife.

My advice to you men is to start behaving like the Lord Jesus Christ in your relationship to your woman, wife, and sweetheart. Then, as God gives you wisdom

and grace to do it, help her with her weaknesses, her needs, and her deficiencies.
Husbands, love your wives, just as Christ also loved the church, and gave
Himself for her; that He might sanctify and cleanse her with the washing
of water by the word, that He might present her to Himself a glorious
church, not having spot or wrinkle or any such thing.[2]

That is not easy. Nobody said it would be. But it is possible through the grace
and power of Jesus Christ our Lord.

---

[2] Ephesians 5:25-27a

Chapter 3
The Married Couple Who Played Hide and Seek

We find the story of "The Married Couple Who Played Hide and Seek" in Genesis 3:8-13.

> And they heard the sound of the LORD God walking in the garden in the cool of the day, and Adam and his wife hid themselves from the presence of the Lord God among the trees of the garden. Then the Lord God called to Adam and said to him, "Where are you?" So he said, "I heard Your voice in the garden, and I was afraid because I was naked; and I hid myself." And He said, "Who told you that you were naked? Have you eaten from the tree of which I commanded you that you should not eat?" Then the man said, "The woman whom You gave to be with me, she gave me of the tree, and I ate." And the Lord God said to the woman,
>
> "What is this you have done?" The woman said, "The serpent deceived me, and I ate."

Imagine, that you're sitting out on your front porch with your spouse on a Dallas evening enjoying the cool evening breeze, and suddenly from inside your house comes the sound of a wild crash and shattering glass, followed by a deafening silence. So you get up and go into your living room, and there you find that your favorite flower vase has fallen to the floor cracked with flowers and pieces of glass scattered all around it. You pause for a moment, and you know that your young son or young daughter is in the house somewhere, but there's not a sound to be heard from anywhere. You engage in a search and eventually open the door to the den. There is your son or daughter, as the case might be, pretending to be deeply absorbed in the TV program they are watching and acting as if nothing out of the ordinary has occurred. So you say to them, "What happened to my favorite flower vase?"

Your son or your daughter says, "It fell off the table, and it broke."

You say, "Well, how did it break? Were you playing in the living room like I always told you not to do?"

Then your son or your daughter says, "The cat ran into the living room, and I went after it. I bumped into the table, and the flower vase fell off and broke." Now, if your son or daughter gave you an answer like this, the reason is that your son is a son of Adam, or your daughter is a daughter of Eve. Here is the answer you probably will not get: "Mom, Dad, I understood what you told me I should not do. I was running around in the living room, and I bumped into the table. I knocked the flower vase off and broke it." If you did not get an answer like that, well that is because from the very earliest years, the children of Adam and Eve are experts at avoiding that long ugly word spelled R-E-S-P-O-N-S-I-B-I-L-I-T-Y. From the earliest years they know how to avoid responsibility.

What happens when we grow up? Do we give up that childish practice? No, we don't. We're better at it than ever because now we've had all these years of ex-perience and practice. Even as the grown-up children of Adam and Eve, we avoid responsibility whenever we can. That leads me to say this: One of the greatest problems that can occur in marriage is marriage partners who avoid responsibility. Or to put it another way, marriage partners who play hide and seek.

Maybe you noticed in our opening Bible passage that on the very day that the first married couple made the first mistake in human history -- it could arguably be called the worst mistake in human history -- on that very day, before it was over, they were playing hide and seek. They were hiding, and God was seeking. Did you notice that the Bible tells us here that "they heard the sound of the LORD God walking in the cool of the day, and Adam and his wife hid themselves" (v 8). Where? "Among the trees of the garden" (v 8). Dumb, don't you agree? Dumb, dumb, dumb! I mean, the Person they were hiding from was the Creator of them and the garden. He was the all-wise, the all-seeing, the all-knowing God. Somehow Adam and Eve figured they could hide from Him behind some trees.

The psalmist knew better, didn't he? Remember his words in Psalm 139:7b-12:

Or where can I flee from Your presence?...

If I ascend into heaven, You are there;

If I make my bed in hell, behold, You are there.

If I take the wings of the morning,

And dwell in the uttermost parts of the sea,

Even there Your hand shall lead me,

And Your right hand shall hold me.

If I say, "Surely the darkness shall fall on me,"

Even the night shall be light about me;

Indeed, the darkness shall not hide from You,

But the night shines as the day;

The darkness and the light are both alike to You.

If I took a spaceship and went all the way to Venus and hid behind the vapors that are supposed to be on the planet Venus, even there God would see me. There is no hiding from the Lord God Almighty, and yet the children of Adam try to do it over, and over, and over again.

There they were, the first man and his wife, hiding from God behind some trees. You know how it used to go when you played hide and seek as a kid? The seeker gets frustrated and says, "Billy, where are you? Cy, where are you?" Well, it's almost as if the all-knowing God is entering into the little thing that Adam and Eve are trying to play with Him, and He says to Adam, "Where are you? Where are you, Adam?"

Adam replies, "Here I am, Lord, right behind this pear tree. Lord, I'm hiding here because I disobeyed You and ate from the fruit of the tree that You told us not to eat from." That's not in our Bibles, is it? Not there at all. Adam says, "I heard Your voice in the garden, and I was afraid because I was naked; and I hid myself" (v 10).

Stop and think about that for a moment. That is an answer that doesn't explain anything, nothing. Had he heard the voice of the LORD God in the garden before?

Obviously, he had because he recognized it, but he'd never hidden before. Furthermore, he had always been naked and he had never been afraid of that before. So Adam's answer to the Lord is a smokescreen, a verbal smokescreen. It's a reason that doesn't give the reason. Don't you see what Adam has done? He's moved from hiding behind the tree to hiding behind empty words.

Let me say to all who are born-again Christians, that although we are saved by the grace of God, we maintain our relationship with God, our harmony with God, and our fellowship with God, only by accepting our responsibility. Remember the words of the apostle John in 1 John 1:6: "If we say that we have fellowship with Him, and walk in darkness, we lie and do not practice the truth." But 1 John 1:9 says, "If we confess our sins, He is faithful and just to forgive us our sins and to cleanse us from all unrighteousness." What does God want of His children? Right up front, He wants the willingness to accept responsibility for the things that we have done wrong. That is something we often fail to do.

Now I can almost hear somebody saying, "Well Zane, I think I already know that. I know we're supposed to accept our responsibility before God, but I thought this book was about marriage. What does that have to do with marriage?" Stay tuned!

Let's go back to the verbal smokescreen that Adam is attempting to employ. God says to him, "Who told you that you were naked? Have you eaten from the tree of which I commanded you that you should not eat?" (v 11) Bingo! Bullseye! Dead right! So Adam says, "You got me, Lord. I admit it. That's exactly what I did. I disobeyed You, and I ate of the tree." Again, that is not what Adam said. What did he say? "The woman whom You gave to be with me, she gave me of the tree, and I ate it" (v 12). Do you see what Adam is doing? He first started by hiding behind a tree, then he continued by hiding behind his own verbal smokescreen, and now he is hiding behind his spouse.

Now ladies, don't relax here. Ladies are every bit as good at this behavior as men are. Avoiding responsibility by hiding behind your spouse is an equal opportunity, full-time occupation, and there are literally thousands and thousands of husbands and wives who have busily engaged in it all over the country -- hiding from God behind your spouse. My thought is that when God gets a little too close to us, when His Word begins to make us a little uncomfortable in our hearts and our consciences, one of the easiest places to hide is not in the shrubs and bushes outside our home, or even in one of the darkest closets in our house. One of the easiest places to hide is behind our spouse.

Can you imagine a marital counseling session that goes like this: Here's a husband and wife who are having real trouble, and they're sitting in the office of the marriage counselor, and the husband says, "Before we start, Mr. Counselor, I want to list my faults as a husband." He lists his faults, and never says one word of criticism about his wife. Then the wife says, "Before we start, Mr. Counselor, I would like to tell you my faults as a wife." She lists all her faults as a wife, and never criticizes her husband at all. The counselor says, "Session over. Go home, and work on your faults." Are there any of you who think there is such a marriage counseling session that occurs like that? If you do, you are not living on the same planet that I'm living on.

Let me tell you what many marriage counseling sessions are like. They are like a slash and burn operation -- slash and burn. The husband says, "My wife does this, and she says this, and she has this attitude." The wife says, "My husband does this, and he says this, and he has this attitude." The counselor is there saying, "What a mess. What a horrendous mess. Where do I start?" Well, maybe you want to say to me, "Zane, you don't understand. I never blame my wife for my faults. I always blame her for hers." Or the wife says, "I never blame my husband for my faults. I always blame him for his." Really? Really?

Let me give you a complete-the-sentence test. The sentence starts, "If it were not for my spouse I would ......" There are lots of options for completing the sentence.

If it were not for my spouse, I would be more dedicated to God.

If it were not for my spouse, I would come to church more often than I do.

If it were not for my spouse, I would read my Bible more often and I would pray harder.

If It were not for my spouse, I would be more involved with the church and I would be serving the Lord more than I am.

The options are almost endless.

Now folks, you don't have to say those words to God. If you say them in your heart, if you think them in your heart, you are hiding behind your spouse. First and foremost, each and every one of us must come to God and fully accept the responsibility for our failures and our sins. Then, as needed, we need to accept them in the presence of our spouse.

Isn't it too bad, that Eve did not have the equal opportunity to blame her husband on this occasion? When God asks her, "What is this that you have done?", what can she possibly say about her husband? Adam has never displeased her from the day she was created. Even on this very day, he has pleased her by eating of the fruit that she herself has eaten of. It would not have been in any credible way for her to pass any blame on to her husband. So she falls back on the excuse of last resort, the last desperate effort to avoid responsibility; she says, "The devil made me do it." "The serpent deceived me, and I ate" (v 13).

May I suggest to you that one of the reasons we find it so easy to blame a husband or wife and hide behind them is because, more often than not, we can make a good case out of it. We can make it sound very plausible. "You know, my husband does this so how can you blame me for it?" Or "You know, my wife, she's like this, and how can you blame me for it?" But this story shows us, that even when we can not hide behind our spouses, if we are determined to hide, we will find something to hide behind. "If you only understood the kind of home I grew up in..." "If you only understood the kind of environment that I work in..." "If you only understood the problems that I have..." And failing all else, "The devil made me do it." As long as we are determined to hide from God, our spouses are a convenient hiding place when we can make it sound plausible.

Did it ever occur to you that after this incident was over, there should have been some apologies exchanged between Adam and Eve? Adam should and could have said to his wife, "Eve, I'm so ashamed that God confronted me with my sin and I tried to blame you. I should never have done that. I'm sorry. It was wrong for me to try to blame you." Eve could and should have said, "Adam, I was stupid enough to believe the lie of the devil, and I ate of that fruit, and then I made it even worse by coming to you and trying to drag you down with me. I'm sorry. I apologize for that." Did Adam and Eve ever have a conversation like that? I don't know. But the only relevant question is: Do you ever have a conversation like that with your spouse, your husband or your wife?

Now you may wonder how Zane knows about this but let me tell you how apologies often go inside a marriage: "Honey, I realize that it wasn't all your fault. I made some mistakes, too." Notice those magical three-letter words all and too. The interpretation of that is: "Some of it really is your fault, you know. I'm certainly not the only one who made mistakes." There is that wonderful fabric softener called mistake -- not sin, mind you, not evil, wicked, or wrong. "I made a mistake."

Now folks, that's not the way we go to God and talk to God, is it? I hope not. I hope you do not go to God and say, "Lord, I made a mistake." You're supposed to say, "Lord, I have sinned." Then God does not say to you, "I'm going to give fifty percent of the responsibility for your sin to you, and fifty percent to your wife," or vice versa. God does not split the difference between us like we often try to split the difference, right? I am one hundred percent responsible for my sin, and you are one hundred percent responsible for yours. The husband is a hundred percent responsible for what he does wrong, no matter what his wife has said or done. The wife is a hundred percent responsible for what she has done, no matter what her husband has said or done.

So here is how an apology ought to work: "Honey, what I said was wrong. What I did was wrong. The attitude I had was wrong. I am sorry, and I apologize for that." Are you making apologies like that to the partner you have married? If you never have an occasion to make that kind of apology to your partner, allow me to suspect that you are not just hiding from your partner. You are probably hiding from God, and you are refusing to acknowledge before God the complete responsibility for what you have done wrong. To put it another way, if you are trying to avoid responsibility by hiding behind your spouse, you are still engaged in the childhood game of hide and seek.

Chapter 4
I'm Ashamed, You're Ashamed

Marriage is honorable among all, and the bed undefiled;
but fornicators and adulterers God will judge.
— Hebrews 13:4

A very good case could be made that the subject of this chapter, physical intimacy in marriage, is one from which a bachelor ought to run away as fast as his two feet will carry him. But an almost equally good case can be made that if I don't discuss this, you may never get a full scriptural treatment of it. So, with perhaps more courage than wisdom, I shall proceed!

While the commonly used word for this subject is sex, I prefer to use the term physical intimacy. God's Word includes several passages that deal with physical intimacy in marriage. I will begin with three passages from this book's Scriptural core, chapters two and three of Genesis.

Genesis 2:21-25:

And the LORD God caused a deep sleep to fall on Adam, and he slept; and He took one of his ribs, and closed up the flesh in its place. Then the rib which the LORD God had taken from man He made into a woman, and He brought her to the man. And Adam said:

"This is now bone of my bones
And flesh of my flesh;
She shall be called Woman,
Because she was taken out of Man."

Therefore a man shall leave his father and mother and be joined to his wife, and they shall become one flesh.

And they were both naked, the man and his wife, and were not ashamed.

Genesis 3:6-11:

> So when the woman saw that the tree was good for food, that it was pleasant to the eyes, and a tree desirable to make one wise, she took of its fruit and ate. She also gave to her husband with her, and he ate. Then the eyes of both of them were opened, and they knew that they were naked; and they sewed fig leaves together and made themselves coverings. And they heard the sound of the LORD God walking in the garden in the cool of the day, and Adam and his wife hid themselves from the presence of the LORD God among the trees of the garden. Then the LORD God called to Adam and said to him, "Where are you?" So he said, "I heard Your voice in the garden, and I was afraid because I was naked; and I hid myself." And He said, "Who told you that you were naked? Have you eaten from the tree of which I commanded you that you should not eat?"

Genesis 3:20-21:

> And Adam called his wife's name Eve, because she was the mother of all living. Also for Adam and his wife the LORD God made tunics of skin, and clothed them.

Suppose you had never heard the story of the temptation and fall of man before, and you get to the place in the story where the devil succeeds in getting the woman to eat the fruit, and she takes the fruit and gives it to her husband. If, not knowing the rest of the story, you were then asked, "What was the first effect of sin on the man and the woman?" you might say, "Well, they fell over dead," because, after all, they had been threatened that eating of the tree of the knowledge of good and evil would lead to death. Or you might say, "They got very, very sick, because what they ate was a piece of fruit that was probably poisoned." Or you might say, "Well, they probably went out of their heads a little bit and started running around the garden wildly, and they were kind of temporarily insane." There are a lot of other things that you might guess.

But, unless you already knew the story, I am betting that you would not guess the correct answer. What was the first effect that sin had on Adam and Eve, as recorded in the Scriptures? Here it is: They became ashamed of their own bodies. May I repeat that? They became ashamed of their own bodies. Notice that right after the man eats, we read, "Then the eyes of both of them were opened, and they knew that they were naked; and they sewed fig leaves together and made coverings" (3:7). They are embarrassed by the fact that they are naked.

A little bit later on, when they hear the voice of the LORD God walking in the garden in the cool of the day, they hide themselves. Then, when God says to Adam, "Where are you?" Adam says, "I heard Your voice in the garden, and I was afraid because I was naked; and I hid myself" (3:10). God's answer is very revealing: "Who told you that you were naked? Have you eaten from the tree of which I commanded you that you should not eat?" "If you are suddenly conscious of your nakedness," says God, "it's probably -- it is certainly -- because you have committed sin."

The first effect of sin on the man and the woman was embarrassment about their own bodies, and that wasn't the way it was before sin, was it? When God made a deep sleep fall on Adam, took out a rib and created the woman, and then brought her to Adam to be his helpmate, Adam was glad to see her, and he called her name Woman. Then we are told that, ". . . they were both naked, the man and his wife, and were not ashamed" (2:25).

So my first point is a very simple one: Shame about our bodies is the effect of sin, not the effect of Creation. It is a very natural extension of that to say that shame about the physical intimacy between husband and wife (which takes place with the body generally unclothed) is a natural outgrowth, the natural result, of the initial effect of sin on the man and the woman. I want to suggest that the children of Adam and Eve have never been able to completely escape their embarrassment about their bodies and about the physical intimacy that takes place in marriage.

Now you may want to say, "Looking at our society and culture today, I don't think that's right. It appears to me that people have lost their shame. So now we get dirty jokes on all these talk shows and sitcoms. Now we have pornographic materials sold at any number of stores. Now we get nudity on the television and movie screens." Our initial impression is that the society has lost its embarrassment.

But let us not jump to conclusions. Sometimes the way human beings hide their basic shame is to get out front and pretend that they are not ashamed. If you take a second look at our culture, you will notice that there are still laws about public nudity that the police enforce. There are still laws about pornographic material and about how old you have to be before it is legal to sell you that material. There are rating systems for movies that warn us about the possibility of nudity and other types of explicit content. So I don't think the culture has outgrown its embarrassment.

One of the most embarrassing experiences of President Bill Clinton's[1] life was almost certainly the public revelation of his affair with White House staffer Monica Lewinsky. In a speech to the nation he admitted to having an inappropriate relationship with Miss Lewinsky. (He did not use the term sexual relationship.) A lot of Americans didn't want to hear about it. They wouldn't talk about it or think about it. Many Americans probably thought, "I wouldn't like my privacy invaded the way the media and the legal investigative committee are invading the president's privacy." This response shows, I think, that our culture still retains a very powerful undercurrent of embarrassment about physical intimacy and about the unclothed human body.

But I'm not particularly concerned with our culture. I'm concerned with Christian couples because this embarrassment that is part of our inheritance from Adam and Eve can invade the bedroom and impair the physical intimacy that should exist between husband and wife.

Many years ago I was talking with a young friend who was getting ready to be married. I was scheduled to perform the ceremony, and I did so. We were talking about the physical intimacy that takes place in marriage. We were not talking about immorality, the improper use of physical intimacy. I will never forget what he said to me. He said, "I know it's a sin, but . . ." I don't remember the rest of what he said

---

[1] William Jefferson Clinton, 42nd President of the United States, 1993-2001

because I was struck by the fact that he was talking about the physical intimacy within a marriage. He said, "I know" -- not I think -- "I know that this is sin." I sat there and thought to myself, "This young man does not understand the Bible, and his opinion about physical intimacy in marriage is the exact opposite of the Bible." You may ask, "How do you know that?" Answer: The Bible tells me so.

This chapter opened with Hebrews 13:4: "Marriage is honorable among all, and the bed [obviously a reference to physical intimacy] undefiled." By contrast, "fornicators and adulterers God will judge." That is unclean; that is legitimately embarrassing; that is something God will deal with. But marriage is honorable, and physical intimacy is not defiled.

When I used to teach kids, one of my favorite questions to ask was, "Who is stricter, God or the devil?" I loved to ask that question because they always got it wrong. Always! They never answered it correctly. They always told me that God was stricter because their image of the devil was that the devil is the person who taps you on the shoulder and says, "Go out and do anything you want to. Break all the commandments. Do what you want to." So the answer I always got was that God is stricter than the devil.

I said, "No, the devil can actually be stricter than God," and then I referred them to
1 Timothy 4:1-3:

> Now the Spirit expressly says that in latter times some will depart from the faith, giving heed to deceiving spirits and doctrines of demons, speaking lies in hypocrisy, having their own conscience seared with a hot iron, forbidding to marry, and commanding to abstain from foods which God created to be received with thanksgiving by those who believe and know the truth.

What do the demons teach? Well, if the devil can't get to you by persuading you to break all the rules and kick all the traces, he's got another method. He tells you, "Physical satisfaction is wrong." Have you ever heard the expression, "It was so wonderful, it was sinful"? That testifies to the innate feeling which human beings have that if it's really, really wonderful, if it's really, really enjoyable, especially as concerns the body, well then something must be wrong with it. God could not intend us to be so happy. But that is not what the Bible teaches at all.

Before man fell into sin, there was absolutely no sense of guilt or shame as the man and woman lived together totally unclothed. I can imagine that physical intimacy between them was the most beautiful thing one could possibly imagine: two people in total harmony, two people in total love with God and with each other, enjoying this wonderful gift that God had given them.

That leads me to my second point: In a Christian marriage, if either party in the marriage approaches physical intimacy with a sense of guilt, that can seriously impair the marriage. Talk to any marriage counselor and I'm quite sure they will tell you what I'm about to tell you because I've heard it from people who have studied the problems that exist in marriage. One of the major problems in many marriages is that the husband and wife are poorly adjusted at the level of their physical intimacy with each other. When there is something wrong in this, which is the most intimate experience a man and a woman can have together, there will be something wrong with the marriage. And because of this poor adjustment, marriages have been known to dissolve and end in divorce.

One of the first things that all Christian couples -- man and woman alike -- should get hold of is that "Marriage is honorable among all, and the bed is undefiled."[2] It is clean in the sight of God. Consider I Corinthians 7:1-5:

> Now concerning the things of which you wrote to me: It is good for a man not to touch a woman. Nevertheless, because of sexual immorality, let each man have his own wife, and let each woman have her own husband. Let the husband render to his wife the affection due her, and likewise also the wife to her husband. The wife does not have authority over her own body, but the husband does. And likewise the husband does not have authority over his own body, but the wife does. Do not deprive one another

---

[2] Hebrews 13:4

[the Greek word for deprive here is a word that can also be translated rob or deform, so another translation could be, "do not rob one another"]

except with consent for a time, that you may give yourselves to fasting and prayer; and come together again so that Satan does not tempt you because of your lack of self-control.

If we really understand that the physical intimacy between a husband and his wife is a gift from God -- it is holy in God's sight -- it's only logical to conclude that we are to give it liberally to our partner in marriage unless it be ". . . with consent [by agreement] that you may give yourselves to fasting and prayer" (v 5). Then, after the time is over, He says, "...come together again, so that Satan does not to tempt you."

So guys, the husband doesn't have this authority in his marriage. He cannot go to his wife and say, "Look, I'm the head of the family. We're not going to be intimate for 30 days so I can fast and pray." He can't do that. That is not his area of authority. He will have to get agreement from his wife. And his wife will also have to get agreement from him. If you do it without the agreement of the other party, you are robbing your spouse.

Now, what really happens in marriages? Well, even us bachelors know some of this. The husband thinks, Ever since I got home from work, my wife has been nagging the life out of me, complaining about this and complaining about that, and now she wants to be intimate. No way. But aloud he says, "I'm sorry, honey. I had a tough day at work and I'm too tired." The husband just robbed his wife, folks. The wife thinks, Ever since he got home he's hardly said a word to me. First, he buried himself in the newspaper and then he spent hours watching the sports on television, and now he wants to be intimate. No way. "I'm sorry, honey. Not tonight. I have a headache." What has the wife done? She has just robbed her husband.

Now, please don't misunderstand me. I know there are times when sensitive husbands and wives will realize, Yeah, my spouse is tired out. He or she really does have a headache. Or, The kids are sick, and we have to be jumping up every five minutes to take care of them. Now, let me make this emphatic: If you say no without having a really, really good reason for saying no, you have not only sinned against your spouse, you've sinned against God. I didn't make this up, folks. This is what the Bible teaches.

So, surprise! When you have physical intimacy with your husband or wife, you are not sinning. It is when you don't that you may be sinning. Now, that leads me to one last observation. Quite obviously that the covering of fig leaves which the man and woman rapidly sewed together for themselves was not quite successful. So when God came into the garden they were embarrassed, and they went behind the trees and shrubs and tried to hide out.

At the end of our story, what do we find? We find that "Also for Adam and his wife the Lord God made tunics of skin and clothed them" (3:21). He was not going to leave them embarrassed. It's possible, of course, that God could have made tunics of skin just appear out of thin air, but neither I nor anyone else thinks He did that. In all probability God had to kill one or more animals in order to get tunics of skin. So even though the man and woman didn't die when they ate the fruit, somebody else died. Because of the sinfulness of man, innocent creatures died that day, and God took their skins to clothe the man and the woman.

Now it has often been pointed out, and I think correctly so, that here we have the first example of animals being killed because of the sin of man. This theme runs all the way through the Old Testament in the sacrificial system. We know that all the animal sacrifices looked forward to the ultimate sacrifice for sin, the Lord Jesus Christ, of whom John the Baptist said, "Behold! The Lamb of God who takes away the sin of the world!"[3]

I want to conclude this chapter by making a very simple suggestion: If you suffer from a sense of shame or guilt or anything like that in the process of physical intimacy, you need to remember the cross of the Lord Jesus Christ. If you are a Christian, when you believed in the Lord Jesus Christ, God washed you of all your sins. He dressed you. He dressed you in the robe of His own righteousness. He covered up everything that you need to be ashamed of. You are free to enter into physical intimacy with your partner because the sacrifice of Christ has covered everything.

---

[3] John 1:29b

Now let's face the facts, shall we? A lot of people, when they get married today, are not having physical intimacy for the first time. They have had it before in situations that God did not approve of, in situations that were wrong. When that has happened, it is very easy to bring into marriage the feeling, "I'm dirty. I'm already dirty." And if the person already thought that physical intimacy is always dirty, they'll feel even dirtier when they are engaged in physical intimacy with their spouse.

So, what is the solution to our embarrassment? May I suggest that it is faith? Just as we are saved by faith in Christ, so we should enter the physical intimacy of marriage with faith: faith, first of all, that our sins are all forgiven by the blood of the Savior; secondly, faith that God's word is true when He says, "Marriage is honorable among all, and the bed undefiled"[4]; and thirdly, faith that in acting as we do with our spouse, we are obeying the Lord, we are doing what is pleasing in His sight.

How many parents, how many husbands and wives, enter into physical intimacy that way? I don't know the answer, but if you do not have this kind of guilt-free experience before God, then the chances are good that you're not believing something God has told you in the Scriptures.

You know, if I were a parent and had kids reaching adolescence, I would want to have a talk with them. If I had a boy, I'd do the talking myself, but if it was a girl, I'd let my wife do the talking. I think the talk should go something like this: "Son, in the years from now on, you're going to find that you have physical feelings and desires that are new to you and strange. They sometimes seem hard to control. The first thing I want to tell you is that there's nothing wrong with these feelings. There's nothing wrong with these desires. That's the way God has made us. He has created us to have these desires.

Now, God wants us to use these desires and satisfy these desires in an appropriate way, and God's way of satisfying these desires is within the framework of marriage. If you try to fulfill these desires outside of marriage, you will find that the results are very bad. You will find that you feel guilty about it. You will find that when you finally do get married, your experience of this with your spouse may be

---

[4] Hebrews 13:4

diminished. It may be tarnished. It may be damaged. So the very best thing you can do is to reserve yourself for the life partner God will give you. And then, within that life partnership, be happy to give this satisfaction to your partner and to enjoy the process of giving."

Now, if you're a parent and that is not your philosophy, how can you talk to your kids like that? You can't. If there's any problem in this area, let's deal with it before God. Make sure that if and when you do talk to your kids, you're not being a hypocrite. Make sure that what you tell them about the proper experience of physical intimacy is the experience you actually accept and believe in and enjoy with your partner.

Bottom line: The next time you are physically intimate with your partner in marriage, say to yourself, "I'm so thankful for this wonderful privilege of giving pleasure to my partner." Don't enter it selfishly. Think in terms of it being a gift that you give to your partner: "I'm so glad that God has privileged me to give this to my partner in marriage."

Then remember what the Bible said, what Jesus said: "It is more blessed to give than to receive".[5] If marriage partners would stop being so selfish, would stop feeling so guilty, and would instead treat this intimacy as a privilege that God has put into their hands to give happiness to their partner, it would not only reshape the experience of physical intimacy, it would immeasurably improve their marriage.

---

[5] Acts 20:35

Chapter 5
No More Fairy Tale

In Ecclesiastes 4:9-12 we read:

Two are better than one,

Because they have a good reward for their labor.

For if they fall, one will lift up his companion.

But woe to him who is alone when he falls,

For he has no one to help him up.

Again, if two lie down together, they will keep warm;

But how can one be warm alone?

Though one may be overpowered by another, two can withstand him.

And a threefold cord is not quickly broken.

Now let's look again at Genesis, chapter 3. In verses 16-19 we read:

To the woman He said:

"I will greatly multiply your sorrow and your conception;

In pain you shall bring forth children;

Your desire shall be for your husband,

And he shall rule over you."

Then to Adam He said, "Because you have heeded the voice of your wife, and have eaten from the tree of which I commanded you, saying, 'You shall not eat of it':

"Cursed is the ground for your sake;

In toil you shall eat of it, all the days of your life.

Both thorns and thistles it shall bring forth for you.

And you shall eat the herb of the field.

In the sweat of your face you shall eat bread,

Till you return to the ground,

For out of it you were taken;

For dust you are,

And to dust you shall return."

Of all the movies I saw when I was a little boy, none of them impressed me more than Walt Disney's famous animated film Snow White. Snow White lived out in a forest in a house that was owned by seven dwarfs. At an early stage of my childhood, I had rubber figures of all seven of the dwarfs and even a rubber figure of Snow White (which was less durable and didn't last as long as the others). To this day I can give you the names of the seven dwarfs in correct order: Doc, Grumpy, Happy, Sleepy, Sneezy, Bashful and Dopey. Every day they walked out and marched to work. Doc was always in the front, and Dopey brought up the rear. And, of course, they sang that delightful song, "Heigh-ho, heigh-ho, it's off to work we go." So they went to work. Then every evening they came marching back in the same order with Doc in front and Dopey behind. This time, of course, they sang "Heigh-ho, heigh-ho, it's home from work we go."

Now all the time they were out working during the day, Snow White was back at the house alone, and she daydreamed about her future. Who could ever forget that beautiful song, "I'm Wishing"? She made a wish beside a wishing well, and of course what she was wishing for was a gallant, handsome prince who would come into her life and sweep her off her feet and carry her away so that she and he could live happily ever after. She also sang the song "Someday My Prince Will Come." Now if you know the story, you know what happened. She ate a poisoned apple and went into a death-like coma from which the seven dwarfs could not rouse her. But one day her prince came, and there she was. When he kissed her, she came back to life again and woke up from her coma. He took her on his horse, and they rode away to live happily ever after.

I would like to suggest that the story of Snow White is a good example of what we could call the fairytale version of marriage. Now when I was a little boy it was still possible to dream about a fairytale marriage. In those days people did not divorce as frequently as they do today. The latest figures, I understand, are that in a given year about 50% of marriages will end in divorce. But when I was a little boy, people stayed together and divorce was kind of a stigma. In fact, it would not have been surprising in my day to have somebody in the neighborhood say, "You see so-and-so over there? He or she is divorced!" So as a little boy -- especially if you lived in a home where the marriage was happy -- imagine that someday a beautiful princess would come into your life. She would be madly sweet and agreeable. We would get married and live happily ever after.

Now things have changed. Back in my day, Ronald Reagan[1] could have never been elected president because he had divorced and remarried. Back in my day, Bob Dole[2] could not have run for president because he also, as I understand, left his first wife and married Liddy[3]. Of course, things have not gotten any better since then, and now we have immorality in the White House. If the polls are to be believed, a lot of people don't think that makes any big difference.

If it is really true that 50% of marriages collapse, that means approximately 50% of the kids who grow up in America come from broken homes. It is very, very hard to have positive ideas about marriage, if you come out of a home where the marriage has been unhappy. I would say, the reality is probably that not too many people actually dream about fairytale marriages.

After I got a little bit older, I realized that fairytale would not necessarily de-scribe even the marriages of people who stayed together. A lot of times people stay together who are in very unhappy marriages with very little love and very little fellowship. They are staying together because society expects it or because of the children or something like that. I want to suggest -- and at least this is good -- that most of us have left behind the idealism and fantasy that sometimes comes to us when we are young, and that as we look forward to marriage, we realize there are no more fairy tales.

Did you know that there has only been one real fairytale marriage in the whole history of the world? That fairytale marriage occurred in the Garden of Eden and

1 Ronald Wilson Reagan was the 40th president of the United States, 1981-1989.
2 Robert Joseph Dole was the Republican presidential nominee in 1996.
3 Elizabeth Mary Alexander Hanford Dole

went on as long as the man and the woman obeyed God and did not fall into sin. Stop and think about it for a moment, if you will. The only two people in the garden were Adam and Eve, and they saw each other all the time. Now I have heard rumors-- since I don't know this firsthand-- that sometimes, when a man retires and he is around the house all the time, the woman wishes he were back at work. Having the guy around the house is a bit much because it maybe interferes with what the wife is used to be doing by herself for a large part of the day.

But think of it, Adam and Eve were the only two people in the garden. They could thoroughly enjoy each other's company. They never had an argument. Neither one of them was ever selfish. They never got mad and fought. Eve never threw pears at Adam, and Adam never threw oranges at Eve. It was perfect. It was wonderful, until sin came.

Then Satan deceived the woman into eating the forbidden tree of the knowledge of good and evil. She immediately went to her husband, and he willingly ate along with her. Then when God came into the garden, they both hid from Him. When they couldn't hide any more, the man, you will remember, quickly passed the buck to his wife. Then the wife quickly passed it on to the serpent, and that left God to address all three parties.

First, He had words of condemnation for the serpent. God then had words directed to Eve and words directed to Adam. As we look at what God said to Eve and Adam, we can understand that God is really saying, "There is no more fairy tale. The fairy tale is over."

I would just like to pause here to say that the fairy tale is over when it comes to marriage. Now you are probably thinking, "Zane, tell me something I didn't know. You know, this is not exactly a hot news flash. If I ever thought that marriage was a fairy tale, I discovered within the first week of marriage that there was no fairy tale. This is a real person I was living with, and the romance, you know, simmered out of sight. Then we settled down to reality." This realization is good because it is very important for us to realize what marriage actually is and what it can be in a world that is now filled with sin, suffering, and death.

Did you notice what God said to Eve? God said "I will greatly multiply your sorrow and your conception. In pain you shall bring forth children" (v 16). Now, I think almost everybody would agree that one of the high points of any marriage is the birth of children. If there is any time when the parents are happiest, it is when the child is born. Yet, as this makes clear, even the process of giving birth to that child who is a delight to the parents, "in pain you shall bring forth children."

There is more than that. God said, "I will greatly multiply your sorrow and your conception." I don't know how long Adam and Eve lived in the Garden of Eden before they sinned. I doubt very much that it was a very short time. I can't imagine them just living there a few days, for example, and then coming into sin. They may have lived there for many months. They may even have lived there for years. But one thing we notice is that, apparently, as long as they were in the garden, Eve never got pregnant; she never produced an offspring.

But remember that in that state of affairs, they were conditioned and programmed to live forever. There was no hurry about giving birth to children, and the reproductive system was probably much, much slower because it was part of the physical makeup of people who potentially could live forever. But now, sin and death had entered the world, and the lifespan had dramatically shortened. God said, "I will greatly multiply your conception." I think this implies that the process of conception and birth is sped up for the woman so that during her few best child-bearing years, she may bear a number of children.

But notice that when He said, "I will greatly multiply your conception," He also said, "I will greatly multiply your sorrow". Now one of the things we all love about mothers is their maternal instincts. Every one of us, I suspect without exception, loved our mother. One of the reasons we loved our mother was because she loved us so manifestly and so tenderly. She was nurturing. She was caring. She was sympathetic. She felt everything that we felt. That is wonderful, but it is also a source of suffering. Yes, the birth of a child is a wonderful and joyful event, but then the life of a child may be something quite different. What happens if the child gets sick? What happens if the child contracts an incurable disease? What happens if the child has an accident that leaves him debilitated? What happens if the child himself grows up and has an unhappy life? Who is it, that has the most sorrow over that? I think it is, without question, the mother. "I will greatly multiply your sorrow and your conception."

I think I learned this best in my own experience when my brother David passed away and I went home to be with my parents. Both of my parents were grieved at the passing of David. Nobody expected the youngest member of the family to be the first to go. My father obviously was deeply grieved, but I very soon learned that my mother grieved in a very definite and specific way. I think it is fair to say it hurt her more to lose David than it hurt my dad, as much as it hurt my dad. I'll never forget something my mother told me on that occasion.

Remember the story where Mary takes the infant Jesus into the temple to be circumcised and the elderly man, Simeon, takes the child Jesus into his arms. One of the things Simeon says to Mary is, "Behold, this Child is destined for the fall and rising of many... Yes, a sword will pierce through your own soul also."[4] Of course, Simeon had referenced the fact that Mary would have to watch her own Son die, and it would be like a sword driven through her heart.

I remember my mother saying to me, "You know, I now understand what Mary felt when Jesus died. It is like a sword going through you." I knew what she was saying, but I knew there was a depth of experience there, a depth of sorrow there, that I could not enter into -- no man probably can enter into --because the woman carries this child to birth, nurtures it and cares for it, and the death of a child is like a sword passing through the heart of a woman. The reality of it is, that even though there is a wonderful and marvelous joy related to the bearing of children, even though there are many joys associated with the rearing of children and the future lives of children, there is nevertheless the solemn and serious reminder that as pregnancies are multiplied for the woman, so also the sorrows are multiplied.

---

[4] Luke 2:34-35a

Then did you notice what God said to Adam? He said, "Cursed is the ground for your sake; in toil you shall eat of it all the days of your life".[5] Remember that before the Fall, Adam was a gardener. That was his occupation. He worked in a perfect world where I assume the fruit trees grew quite naturally. There was no problem in having to fertilize anything and probably no problem with having to prune the weeds. If I may say so, Adam had the softest job in human history. He probably could go somewhere and say, "I don't feel like pruning anything in the garden at this point. Besides, it doesn't need pruning. I don't feel like checking out the trees. I checked them out yesterday, and there is nothing to check out." He had it great. He had it perfect.

But now the fairy tale is over. "You, as the husband, will have to work. And the ground from which you will have to grow your food will no longer cooperate with you. In toil you shall produce fruit from the ground. Not only that," said God, "the ground is going to produce thorns and thistles. As you work with the ground, the thorns and thistles are going to cut you and gash you. You will bleed in the work that you do. In the sweat of your face, you shall eat bread all the days of your life until you return to the dust from which you were taken."[6]

Now, maybe I am giving away a Men's Club secret here, but hopefully the men will forgive me. When men get together to talk and share their complaints with each other, you know what their chief complaint normally is? Relax, ladies, it is not you. Of course, there are things at home that they do complain about. But get a typical group of men together, and you know what they are going to complain about? Their jobs. "My, the hours on my job are absolutely inhuman. I have to get up at 2:00 am, and I get out at 5:00 pm. The boss that I work for is dreadful. I mean, he is so demanding, and he never appreciates anything. My paycheck is so pitiful compared to the work that I do. You ought to see the people that I work with. And there is a person that sits next to me and I cannot stand that person. I don't know why they don't fire him." And on and on it goes. Why? Because as far as work is concerned, we are not in Eden anymore. We are in a fallen world, in a world that is marred by death and sin.

---

[5] Genesis 3:17
[6] Paraphrase of Genesis 3:17-19

To illustrate, let me tell you a little about my dad's career. My dad never finished high school because he came from a large family and had to work to help the family support itself. He started out at a relatively low level. When I first became conscious of such things as work, he was working for the War Department which is today called the Defense Department. He had entered it probably at the clerical level or something like that, but my father worked himself up the chain. Eventually he was invited to move from the Baltimore area to the Chambersburg area to become the head of personnel at the Letterkenny Army Ordnance Depot. He was the chief of personnel. He was later promoted to what amounted to be the executive assistant to the commanding officer of the depot. To put it another way, my father was the top civilian of that depot and the best paid civilian. He was a success in his career. (By the way, I found out through many sources that he was greatly admired for his integrity. He was an honest man. If somebody didn't like him and my dad knew that he didn't like him, my dad would bend over backwards to be fair with that guy. We used to kid my father and say, "You know, Dad, if we had to work for you it would be better to be your enemy than to be your friend.)

But while my dad was a very successful person in his career, you know what I never heard him say? I don't ever remember hearing him say, "I love my work. I like what I am doing." Never once, I can recall hearing him say that. What I can recall is all the times that he brought a whole stack of papers home from work. See, he dealt with people during the day but had no time to do paperwork, so he had to do it at night and sometimes very late into the night.

And talk about working with people! If you are the head of personnel, believe me, all these big problems in personnel come in your direction. On top of that, all the people who work under you are not always angels, and you have to worry about how they are performing their jobs. Being an executive assistant to the commanding officer, he had the misfortune of running up against the Army's system of putting a colonel in command of the depot for a couple of years, and then putting another colonel in command for a couple of years, and then another. Once or twice, he got a nice colonel. Other times he got really mean Army men, hard to work with.

My dad usually wound up winning the respect of the commanding officer.

I remember one colonel in particular that Dad would come home telling us about, "Colonel Coffee," who was described as coffee because of his bitterness. Dad had a hard time working with Colonel Coffee at first, but later Colonel Coffee came to respect my dad's integrity and work ethic and they became friends. But even though my dad enjoyed success, he never once said, "I like my work." He retired at 55, which is one of the perks of government service. He retired at 55, at the earliest possible moment, I might add, with a very nice pension.

My dad's experience is an experience that is typical of so many men. Yes, they have to work. Yes, they have to sustain their families. But it is hard work, maybe not manually hard work, but sometimes emotionally hard work. Then there are all the "thorns and thistles" that jam your energy at work, that make it so very, very difficult.

"Well," you say, "all you have told us so far is how hard it is for the woman and how hard it is for the man -- the woman whose focus is on her children and the man whose focus is on his work. It is hard, and there is no fairytale existence anymore. Why does God make it like that? Is God just mad at everybody because of what Adam and Eve did, and so He says, 'All right, I want everybody to have a hard time. I am just going to see to it that women have a hard time and men have a hard time.'?" Well, I don't think that's the reason for it at all, which brings me back to Snow White.

Has it ever occurred to you that Walt Disney never made Snow White 2? You know why? It would not have made a good movie. I mean, can you imagine what Snow White 2 would have been like? Here are Snow White and the charming prince. They live in this wonderful palace. They can wake up anytime they want to. The servants take care of everything. They go downstairs, and the servants have breakfast on the table. Of course, if they have a child, he is a perfect child who grows up and behaves and obeys his parents. They have nothing better to do at night than stroll their lovely gardens under the light of the moon and enjoy their marriage together. It would make a terrible movie. Dullsville, USA! Boring!

You know that the nature of human beings is such that if we did not have any troubles, if everything were smooth, we would soon get bored. That would only be the best of it because, you see, when people don't have problems and troubles they also deteriorate as people and become lazy. They become self-indulgent. They become selfish. We are kind of all those things anyway by nature but having everything go our way all the time would make us even worse.

I think it is obvious that now as sinners who live in a fallen world of sin, it would not be good for us to not have problems. It would not really be good for us to have marriages that were absolutely perfect from day one to the end of the line. In fact, remember what James says in the first chapter of James. He says, "Count it all joy when you fall into various trials, knowing that the testing of your faith produces patience. But let patience have its perfect work, that you may be perfect and complete, lacking nothing."[7]

One of the major reasons God gives us a life and a marriage experience that is not absolutely free from suffering and hardship, from woes and sorrows, is because if we will respond to these things in a biblical way, if we respond to them in faith toward God, it can make us a better person. It can make you a better husband if you are a man. It can make you a better wife if you are a woman.

"Well," you say, "that is true of everybody, so what advantage does the married person have? I mean, Zane, you are single and you have troubles too. So, you know, you just double your trouble if you get married." (I'm talking as another bachelor might talk.) No, that is not the case. Actually, it is much better to be married.

One of the things that we learn from the passage from Ecclesiastes that opened this chapter is that two are better than one. Two are better than one. You see, in this wicked world of toil and suffering and sorrow, two are always better than one. One reason the writer of Ecclesiastes gives for that is "because they have a good reward for their labor" (v 9). You know, if I work hard, produce something, and bring it home, who is there to appreciate it but me? If I get a raise in salary, who enjoys the benefits of my salary? Me. It is much happier to be able to share the fruits and rewards of labor with somebody else, your partner in life.

---

[7] James 1:2-4

Then the writer of Ecclesiastes says, "For if they fall, one will lift up his companion. But woe to him who is alone when he falls" (v 10). Now things happen, don't they? Sometimes we get really big falls in our lives. Well, if we have a partner who can pick us up, encourage us, get us back on the way, that is a wonderful, wonderful blessing to have. The writer then says, "Again, if two lie down together, they will keep warm; but how can one be warm alone?" (v 11). You can turn up the heat in the home, but you never get rid of, shall we call it, the coldness of being alone. It is a wonderful blessing and privilege to have somebody there who is your life mate, who makes your life warmer, who makes your life more pleasant because they are there. "If two lie down together, they will keep warm."

And finally the writer of Ecclesiastes says, "Though one may be overpowered by another, two can withstand him" (v 12). Both husband and wife sometimes find not only problems confronting them, but people confronting them. When your husband finds this absolutely impossible boss that he has to face every day of his life and he comes home, how wonderful it is to have a sympathetic ear from his wife. She supports him. She encourages him. She says, "Keep at it. He's wrong. You are doing the best you can." Same thing with the wife. She runs into problems with other people, and the husband can do the same thing for her.

What I am saying here is that because we do live in a fallen world, a world of sin and sorrow and suffering and death, marriage is a wonderful, wonderful privilege. I want you to understand that. I do not have it myself; I think that has been God's will for me. But I certainly recommend and commend marriage because the advantages are tremendous, provided that in the marriage are partners who fill the role of partner. That both partners stand together and share the fruits of their labor together. That one partner is there to pick the other partner up when the partner falls. That both partners are there to keep their hearts warm with intimacy and closeness. That both partners are there to combat outside opposition and the troubles that arise.

You know that over the years, I've talked to a lot of couples who are having marital problems, and when I listen to them, as somebody says in the movie Casablanca, "I'm shocked, shocked." You know why? Because usually, each partner is telling me all the things that are not done for them by the other partner. "He/she does not, did not, etcetera, etcetera, etcetera." How much better it would be if each partner were focused, not on what the other partner is doing for them, but on what they are contributing to the partnership. You know, if each partner would only take a truly unselfish view of marriage, I am convinced that 50 to 75 percent of all problems that exist in marriage would resolve themselves, just because the partners learn to be supportive and unselfish.

I am going to close with a story about my mother and dad. In the closing years of my dad's life, he was very, very infirm. He was, I think, legally blind. He virtually could not do a single thing by himself. He had to get up at night and go to the bathroom numerous times, as old people often do, and my mother had to get up with him every time and go to the bathroom with him. It wouldn't be too long into my visit with them, that my father would say, "You have a real crock for a husband." But my mother didn't look at it that way. She didn't look at it that way at all.

In fact, one of the most moving things she ever said to me took place on my last visit with her (after my dad had gone home to be with the Lord), "I know that Z.C. (my father) is happy now. These large problems that I have, for his sake, I wouldn't want him to be back here." Then she added, "If it was only up to me, I would have him back just the way he was." Because she had centered her life on supporting him in the declining years of his health, she was amazing.

Another thing that she said to me was, "Zane, I did my best to take care of Z.C, but I don't think I did a very good job." And I said to my mother, "I think you did a wonderful job. I am proud of you. I think those years were the finest years of your career as a wife." I don't remember exactly what she said to me, but she said something like, "Thank you."

My mother lived to support my father. If it were the other way around, my dad would have done exactly the same thing. He would have been there for her and supported her. That is the way marriage really ought to be. Remember what Jack

Kennedy[8] said in his inaugural address. He said, "Ask not what your country can do for you. Ask what you can do for your country." So I would ask every married person reading this to ask yourself, not what your spouse can do for you, but what you can do for your spouse.

---

[8] John Fitzgerald Kennedy, 35th President of the United States, 1961-1963

Chapter 6
A Helper Comparable to Him

Two are better than one, because they have a good reward for their labor.

Ecclesiastes 4:9

The account of the first marriage on Earth as recorded in Genesis, chapters two and three, has served as the scriptural core for each chapter of this book. The final chapter is no exception. We begin with Genesis 2:15, 18-24:

[15]Then the Lord God took the man and put him in the garden of Eden to tend and keep it...

[18] And the LORD God said, "It is not good that man should be alone; I will make him a helper comparable to him." Out of the ground the LORD God formed every beast of the field and every bird of the air, and brought them to Adam to see what he would call them. And whatever Adam called each living creature, that was its name. So Adam gave names to all cattle, to the birds of the air, and to every beast of the field. But for Adam there was not found a helper comparable to him.

And the LORD God caused a deep sleep to fall on Adam, and he slept; and He took one of his ribs, and closed up the flesh in its place. Then the rib which the LORD God had taken from man He made into a woman, and He brought her to the man.

And Adam said,

> "This is now bone of my bones
> And flesh of my flesh;
> She shall be called Woman,
> Because she was taken out of Man."
> Therefore a man shall leave his father
> and mother and be joined to his wife,
> and they shall become one flesh.

Quite a few years ago when I was still teaching on the seminary faculty, I used to go out frequently to lunch with several fellow teachers, and we always had a good time solving all the problems of the seminary and the world over lunch. But one semester came when the schedule makers did not accommodate us very well on the basis of our class schedules, and we were going to have to eat lunch at different times. So one of my faculty friends said to me, "Even though I won't be eating with you, I would be glad to come out with you when I can, because I know how awful it is to eat alone." Now the thought that was going through my mind at the time was, "That's very nice, but I love to eat alone!" I love to eat with people, too, of course, but if I eat alone, which I frequently do, I also have a good time because I often take a magazine or a book or something else that I want to read, and I enjoy myself reading. So while I appreciated my friend's concern for me, it didn't exactly fit my particular situation.

I remember another faculty friend saying to me, "I just couldn't stand to come home to an empty house and four walls." And the thought that was going through my mind was, "I love to come home to an empty house and four walls." I make my living teaching people, and I talk to people all day long, so it's great to come home and not have to talk to anybody, not have to hear how their day went or tell them how my day went. I can settle down, take a nap, turn on the TV, or read the newspapers or magazines and have a great time all by myself in a house that has nobody in it but myself.

Now maybe by this time you're thinking, "Well, Zane must be the exception to the statement God made about Adam when He said, 'It is not good for man to be alone.' " Well, I'm not so sure I'm an exception to that, because the question I want to raise is: When God said that, did He mean it's not good for a man to go home to an empty house or not have somebody to eat lunch with, or did He mean more than that? Did you notice that when He said, "It is not good for man to be alone,"[1] He did not then go on to say, "I will make him a companion"? He didn't say that. Now undoubtedly He did make man a companion. But what He actually said was, "I will make him a helper comparable to him."[2]

---

[1] Genesis 2:18a
[2] Genesis 2:18b

Have you ever stopped to think about those words, "a helper comparable to him"? After reading that God said that, the next thing we read is that God has made the animals, and He brings them to Adam, and Adam gives names to all the animals. When he's finished naming all the animals, we are told in verse 20, "But for Adam there was not found a helper comparable to him." I think it is obvious that each of these animals was brought to Adam not only for the task of naming them, but for Adam to consider whether any of these creatures could be what he needed to keep from being alone. Now you may say, "How can that be? Since man cannot talk to the animals and the animals can't talk to man, they couldn't possibly have been good companions for him."

Are you sure of that? Have you ever stopped to think that in Genesis, chapter 3, when the serpent, who "was more cunning than any of the beast of the field" came into the garden and said to the woman, "Has God indeed said, 'You shall not eat of every tree of the garden'?"[3], the woman didn't say, "Eek! You're talking! Where did you get the ability to talk? How can you be communicating with me? What's going on here?" She doesn't say that, does she? She carries on a conversation with the serpent as if, "This is not the first time I've talked to an animal."

Do you know the story of Balaam's donkey, found in Numbers, chapter 22? Balaam is riding his donkey. God is angry at Balaam because he is going to meet with Balak, who wants Balaam to curse the children of Israel. On three separate occasions, as Balaam travels along, the Angel of the LORD stands in the road with a drawn sword.[4] The first two times, only the donkey sees the angel, and when the donkey turns aside to avoid the angel, Balaam whacks the animal in frustration. The third time the angel appears, the donkey just lies down with Balaam on top of it, and this time Balaam beats the donkey with his staff. Then, to our amazement, the donkey says, "What have I done to you, that you have struck me these three times?"[5] Balaam is very angry – he may have been surprised, but he's mainly angry – and he says, "Because you have abused me. I wish there were a sword in my hand, for now I would kill you!" So the donkey said to Balaam, "Am I not your donkey on which you have ridden, ever since I became yours,

---

[3] Genesis 3:1
[4] Numbers 22:22-30
[5] Numbers 22:22-28

to this day? Was I ever disposed to do this you?" And Balaam says, "No."[6] Then the Lord opens Balaam's eyes and he sees the Angel of the LORD. My point is that the donkey talks to him.

I suspect very strongly that many, if not most, of the animals -- perhaps all of them -- could talk at the time God brought them to Adam to get named, and that they lost the capacity to talk as a result of the Fall. It is an interesting possibility that in the kingdom of God we may be able to talk to the animals. We will see. But in any case, I do not think it is very likely that God brought all these animals to Adam and that none of them could communicate with him. Even if they could communicate with him, it seems that none of them provided Adam with what he needed.

I am going to discuss the phrase, "a helper comparable to him." [7]Let's start with the word helper. As I have already said, God did not say, "It is not good for man to be alone. I will make him a companion." Neither did God say, "It is not good for man to be alone. I will make him a lover." And God did not say, "It is not good for man to be alone. I'll make him a dishwasher, or somebody who will keep house." There were no dishes to wash in the Garden of Eden and no house to keep. I think it is significant that what God wants man to have is a helper.

Now I suggested in first chapter of this book that the obvious application of the woman being a helper is that the man had a job to do. He had a job to do in the garden. God created the man, set him in the Garden of Eden, and gave him the responsibility of tending the garden and taking care of it. In Eve, Adam has a helper to help him with the job God has given him. I made the point in Chapter 1 of this book that one of the major roles of the woman in a marriage is to help the man carry out his responsibilities for God, to be his helper in the work that God has called the man to do. He may not be called to preach, but there are various things that each and every man can and should do for the Lord.

---

[6] Numbers 22:29-30
[7] Genesis 2:18b

Each of us has a gift, and the woman is to be her husband's helper in that respect. That is a very important role, indeed. Why is it important? Well, stop and put yourself in Adam's place for a minute. He's there in the garden without Eve. Now, I don't know what was necessary to do in a garden where there was nothing going wrong because there was no sin yet, but there was something that Adam had to do to tend the plants and cultivate the garden. When it's all over, he looks around and he says, "Good job, but so what? I'm doing it. I suppose God appreciates it. It's beautiful, but if I'm doing it just for me, how can I really enter into the value and pleasure of doing it?" I don't know whether he felt that way or not, but that brings us back to Ecclesiastes 4:9 "Two are better than one, because they have a good reward for their labor."

Now Eve comes into the garden. She does her thing and Adam does his thing and then, at the close of the day, Adam and Eve stand there and say, "Hmm. That's pretty. Don't you appreciate that?"

"Yes, I appreciate that and my, you did a good job on the gladiolas."

"And, Adam, you did a good job on the peach tree."

They multiply their satisfaction -- their reward for their labor -- by the fact that they are able to enjoy it and appreciate it together.

You know, my dad did not enjoy his job as the chief of personnel at the Letterkenny Ordnance Depot where he worked for many years. But almost as soon as he retired, he started a vegetable garden. My dad loved to get out in his garden, cultivate it, and grow corn, string beans, tomatoes and whatever else he decided to grow. He fought an ongoing war with the chipmunks who were determined to take advantage of what he produced. During Dad's retirement years, my mother and father would go outside during the daytime. My mother was not particularly interested in the vegetable garden, but she was interested in flowers. While my father cultivated the vegetable garden, my mother took care of the flowers, and they had a good-looking yard. Then they enjoyed the fruits of their labor together because when they brought in my dad's corn or tomatoes, they ate it together. If my mother brought in a bouquet, they could both enjoy it together. They had a good reward for their labor.

Now if you ask me, cultivating a vegetable garden is Dullsville, USA. I can't think of anything more boring than growing a vegetable garden. But whenever I went home to visit my parents, I knew I was in for the grand tour. My dad was going to take me out in the garden, and he was going to show me, plant by plant, what he was growing. I once took my friend Luis up to visit, and I believe my dad took him out once or twice to see the vegetable garden. Then of course, when they fed me at night, my mother would say, "This corn comes from your father's garden" or "These green beans were grown by your dad." They were good, but I often thought to myself, "I will never, ever retire to a house and start a vegetable garden." However, that was their thing, and they loved it. They enjoyed it together, and they had a good reward for their labor because they shared the pleasure of working together in the yard.

I am wondering whether the husbands and wives who are reading this book have ever thought of the whole process of marriage as a sharing of labor. First of all, couples normally have kids and, as we all know, there are certain things that mothers do better for kids than dads do, and certain things that dads do better for kids than mothers do.

We know how important it is for mothers and dads to do the right thing for their kids so that the kids grow up to be the right kind of people. All through the years that you're raising your children, both parents have to think of the ways in which they can serve God. If you do not serve God in front of your children, your children are not going to learn from you how to serve God. They may learn it from somebody else down the line, but they should learn it from you in your home. They should see Mom and Dad love God, and Mom and Dad enjoy the Bible.

I have often said that one of the things I learned from my father was to pray about everything. He taught me a lot of lessons. I cannot even begin to list all the lessons that my dad taught me, but that is probably the most important thing. I learned that you pray about everything. My dad prayed about everything, and there is no estimating how valuable that is to children. So you have to be serving the Lord all along the way. If Mom and Dad are successful in raising their kids in the fear and admonition of the Lord, don't you think that is a wonderful joy to share between husband and wife?

Now in my church, there are a number of parents who have seen that their older children are not walking with the Lord. So each month we have a parents' prayer meeting. If you have already raised or nearly raised your kids, and they are not really walking with the Lord, it is going to take a different kind of work to getting them back, and that work is prayer. I am always glad when I see both husband and wife together at the parents' prayer meeting, praying for their children.

After the children are gone, husband and wife ought to consider what other things they have to do together that are very important. When your children are gone, you still need to be serving the Lord. So I'm saying to the parents reading this, "What are you up to doing together? If your children are out of the nest, what are you doing together? What are your objectives together? Are you working together for God? Are you doing something for God? Are you serving in the church in the roles that He wants you to serve? That's the question, isn't it?" It's not good for a man to have to do it by himself. He needs a helper to help him do his best for God.

The second phrase in Genesis 2:18 is comparable to him. He needs a helper comparable to him. Now I want you to notice that it doesn't say he needs a helper identical to him. Don't you agree that it would be bad if your mate was absolutely identical to you? I once lived on the 16th floor of a high-rise apartment. I shall never forget a pair of elderly men who lived together there. They were twins and looked almost identical to each other. I couldn't tell them apart. It was my understanding that neither of them had ever been married, and I must say they were not too extremely friendly. If you talked to them, you might get a very slight acknowledgement that you had just greeted them, but that is about all. Maybe they were happy, but they were kind of like clones of each other: They were too much alike.

I think that men and women can thank the Lord that they are not identical; they are just comparable to each other. Now, the animals that God brought to the man were radically different from him. Even though the serpent could talk, who would want to have a serpent as their bosom buddy? Who would want a donkey as their bosom buddy? Even if Balaam did talk briefly to his, we do not want to spend a lot of time talking to a donkey. But the woman was like him, and yet at the same time there were physical, emotional, and psychological differences. We can see the wisdom of

God in this: God knew man needed a helper who, though not identical with him, was comparable to him and who complemented, therefore, his own weaknesses and deficiencies with her strengths and skills.

I would like to suggest that the next time you are by yourself for a few minutes, instead of thinking about all the things in your partner that annoy the daylights out of you -- which is pretty easy to think about and consume your time with -- think of all the strong points your partner has that you do not have. I would be greatly surprised if you could not pinpoint some very real strengths your partner possesses that you do not possess. Then thank God for giving you a partner with those strengths and make up your mind to take advantage of being married to this partner and learn from their strengths.

Now I do hope husbands and wives talk to each other about disciplinary problems with their children. I hope they have their act together so that they present a united front. There is nothing worse than one parent saying one thing to the kid and the other parent saying something different. That is chaotic and very damaging for the children. You need to get your act together.

However, if the husband and wife are sitting together and the kid has done something wrong, the dad perhaps feels, "They need to learn a lesson from this, and we need to exercise a discipline that will really communicate this lesson." The mother, being the sympathetic person that mothers usually are, may say, "Yes, that's true. But I think I understand why our child did what they did, and I think we ought to take that into consideration." What happens next? Well, in some families what happens is that the man says, "We're gonna do it my way. We're gonna discipline my way." And the wife says to herself, "OK, but as soon as I get a chance with the kid, I'm gonna communicate my own message to them." Now what they should do is to merge their points of view into an acceptable discipline that takes into consideration, perhaps, the weaknesses in the child that the mother feels, and takes into consideration the father's view that the child should learn a lesson.

Do you see what I'm saying? Husbands and wives can

cannot do it by being on a two-track program -- the husband is ᴜ

wife is off this way, and you are kind of like two ships passing in the oceₐ.

You need to get your act together. You need to cooperate with each other and to incorporate the strengths of each into the way that you handle and discipline your children.

I close with a famous nursery rhyme: "Jack Sprat could eat no fat, his wife could eat no lean, and so between the two of them, they wiped the platter clean." Jack Sprat couldn't eat any of the fat part of the meat, and his wife couldn't eat any of the lean part. I imagine Jack Sprat as a thin, skinny old man, and his wife as a stout woman because she ate only the fat and he ate only the lean. But this was a cooperative venture, so when they had a piece of meat on the table in front of them, Jack Sprat ate his part, and the wife ate her part, and the platter was clean, and no food was wasted. Isn't that great?

Well, I do not know what is on your platter as a couple but let me suggest that to clean up whatever is on your plate -- I'm speaking figuratively here -- you need to work together. The husband needs to do the part he does well, and the wife needs to do the part she does well, and between the two of you, you can wipe that platter clean.

It is true that there are some advantages to being single. However, because I am single, I have to turn to different people to provide some of the benefits that married people get very naturally from one another. I've often thought that a preacher is very fortunate if he has a sympathetic wife who will go home with him and, at an appropriate time, say to him, "You know, such and such an illustration was really confusing, and I didn't follow it. I just wonder if everybody followed it." Or, "You seemed to get lost in point three, and I got lost with you." You have no idea how valuable that kind of input can be, and I regret that I do not have somebody who does that with me on a regular basis. That's just one illustration of many things I could mention where the single man labors under many disadvantages simply because he does not have a helper comparable to him -- an in-house helper who loves him, wants the best for him, and is willing to give him her honest and open counsel.

ne Lord in the church, give him the benefit

ɾ you are not trying to cut him down to size, you

ɾe. That is the important thing. Then you are a real

Corinthians 7:32-35 Paul recognizes some very concrete

ɾe. But it is still, in my opinion, not good for man to be alone

bɾ   ɾmething missing from the single life that the individual with a

happy aɾ   ɾcessful marriage has. "Each one has his own gift from God," says

the Scripture, "one in this manner and another in that".[8] God knows what is best

for each of us, and for most of us, marriage is best.

---

[8] 1 Corinthians 7:7

Made in the USA
Monee, IL
18 April 2021

65040609R00046